LOST AND FOUND

Life after a Stroke

Including
PATHFINDER

KARI THOMASON

All Rights Reserved.

No part of this book may be reproduced, stored in a retrieval system or transmitted in any form or by any means without the prior written permission of the publisher, except in case of brief quotations embodied in critical articles and review to be printed in a newspaper, magazine or journal. Member of educational institutions and organizations wishing to photocopy any of the work for classroom use, or authors, artists and publishers, who would like to obtain permission for any material in the work, should contact the author.

ISBN: 9798389996427
First Edition: April, 2023
Contact Information: 07584498050

E-mail: karithomason02@gmail.com

LOST AND FOUND Inc PATHFINDER Copyright©
2023 **KARI THOMASON**

ACKNOWLEDGMENT

I would like to dedicate this book to George and Mildred (They know who they are) especially Mildred, a true Angel. She came to me as a befriender from church. That was a year ago (Definitely not a runner) and she keeps coming back for more......God is good.

To their daughter who has a voice like an Angel. When she plays her flute in church, it always soothes my ruffled feathers and calms my often restless spirit.

To all stroke survivors there is life after a stroke. You've got this. You are not alone.

Table of Contents

LOST AND FOUND 1

ACKNOWLEDGMENT 3

FOREWORD 7

    WHO AM I? 10

    QUESTIONS.....NO ANSWERS? 13

    WHAT....WHEN.....HOW? 15

    WHERE??? 17

    EMOTIONS 19

    LET ME REST 20

    HEY! JUST ME!!! 21

    SID 23

    THE CHALLENGE 25

    I PRAY 27

    ANGER 29

    IS IT REHERSHAL OR TEST? 30

    ANOTHER 32

    DARKNESS V LIGHT 33

    CONFUSION 35

    A BIG DEAL 37

    I'M THINKING 39

    THANK YOU TO THE BEST STROKE TEAM 41

PATHFINDER 43

    IN BETWEEN THE LINES 44

ENOUGH	46
YOU'RE NOT LISTENING	48
WHY?	51
THE BOTTOM LINE LORD......?	53
BORROWED TIME	55
CHASING A RAINBOW	57
CHANGE	58
BUTTONS	60
TIME OUT	63
DIFFERENCES	65
THE STOPWATCH	69
MY AWESOME GOD	72
MY COMMITMENT	74
THE COMPASS	76
THE KEYRING	78
WONDERING	80
BLIND SPOT	81
A PEP TALK	83
HE'S ALWAYS WITH ME	85
NEVER	89
OPEN	90
I AM TRYING	91
TO ANYONE WHO'S LISTENING?	92
VOTE OF THANKS	94

ABOUT THE AUTHOR 95

FOREWORD

Have you or a loved one experienced a stroke?

Just as Kari had struggled to cope with the aftermath of stroke, there are many other people who struggle just as she had struggled with the understanding, the management, and the journey of recovery.

Kari is a woman with a big heart and big love.
In her words, she says; you are not alone. She believes there is an endless and infinite amount of love in the world. She hopes all of us feel inclined to agree and that we access the infinite supply of love that she believes will surge from within us as a new light into the world.

Kari believes Love is the greatest gift and it should be passed on to others who need love. She has two grown children, Shane and Trudi and four grand children, Ben, Max, Phoenix and Quinn.
Kari says: It is all about family. Family, over the years has been a huge support system in difficult times.

During my exchanges with Kari, she told me that her family is the world to her and she is proud to be a part something so wonderful.

Through the darkest times, she was not alone. She struggled with her faith and hopes her stories become an inspiration to many other people around the world. Her writing has always being her therapy and her Prose Poems reflect her journey with the good, the bad and the ugly.

Lost but found provides a detailed insight into the struggles that have rocked Kari's world. Her life after a stroke presents Kari's story in this book which takes us on a critical journey and provides insights on the physical, emotional and spiritual struggles that comes with such a life altering event. During her recovery she also faced challenges to her Christian faith which led to a series of poems under the second collection called Pathfinder.

As Kari writes, she expresses both the experiences of Stroke Recovery and her struggles of faith. She asks: Am I dead or alive? Why can't I remember how I got here? The hospital bed isn't like the one I have at home.

Her sense of humour, and that of her befriender, church members and family has been her support system. She says: when I can't find my sense of humour, the love bestowed restores my hope.

Kari's life dream is to become an example and a shining light to the next generation. She has become a big energy that ignites a new vision through her writing. She says: why can't I get my words out? They are stuck in my head and in my heart. She is at the start of a new dream, a new mission and at many times, she propels herself with courage.

Kari is a big energy for the young people. 'Alatishe' is one of those whom Kari has influenced positively over the years and he is proud to acknowledge her. Kari is one of those who inspired the Alatishe's evolution and his numerous revolutionary titles.

Where are you Lord, Kari Asks? Within the struggles, her emotions were entangled and detached.

Within the thought silencing moments, she prays and she does so with a huge love for humanity.

Kari continues to thank the best stroke team through her lethal pen. She says: You put the pride back. You have helped me walk that extra mile.

Alatishe Kolawole.

Founder,
The Generator International

WHO AM I?

Who am I?
Who did I used to be?
Who is the doctor
now talking to?
Am I still ME?

Is he telling someone
I had a bad stroke?
When he looks directly at me,
I must've done something
really bad.

Is this pain my punishment?
Is this the way my life now will be?
The doctor reassures me
that I haven't done anything wrong.

So I ask him,
Is this some kind of joke?
I don't even know
how I got here.

Are you sure I have had a stroke?
I couldn't stop the tears
from falling when I hear the news.

Why did I feel so weak?

LOST AND FOUND ...Life After a Stroke

You've made a mistake,
I tearfully told him.
Stroke victims, they can't speak.

Each individual is different.
No two are the same.
Some may lose the use of their limbs.
Some can't remember their name.
Some have to learn to walk again.
Almost childlike, they begin.
Their recovery can be slow and long.

The fighting Spirit kicks in.....
But I can't remember anything
I don't even know how I got here?
All I know is my heart and soul
is totally full of fear.

The doctor smiled
and held my hand.
We are not your enemies.
We are your friends.

Tell me Kari, do you have Faith?
If you do, then you must believe
that this is not a punishment.

Now SMOKING:
That thought with you I shall leave........

Every thought that you are thinking now
is normal after a stroke.
I have trained and worked
in this field a long time.
I class myself as an honest bloke.

Get some rest,
I will see you tomorrow.

Any questions,
Don't be afraid to ask the staff.
Even if you ask the same one
over and over again.

It's all part of the stroke.
They will not laugh
We are all here to help you on your new path.

QUESTIONS.....NO ANSWERS?

I have travelled down on Lola.
My mobility wheels
down to the main lounge
to do some writing.
Yet, strange is all I feel.
I'm looking now
at my old notes.
I ask, why do none of them
make sense?
Well, I believe they must have
at some point.
Right now, I feel so dense.
I am seriously wondering if I'm losing it.
Did my stroke do more damage
than I first thought?
Yes, it did.
It drove me back to school.
I learnt to walk again.
How am I feeling
right at this moment?
I feel frustrated.
Anger seems to come nowhere.
I'm trying to keep a lid on it
as best I can.

Confused, Oh yes!
DEFINITELY

It's 7pm, New Year's Day.
I can't believe I have
made it through
to another year.
I was told I wouldn't
Make it to 55 years old.
At 61 years young,
I am still here.
Now, my stroke was
3 years ago.
They said I had two
bleeds on the brain.
Though, they said there
was no damage to my brain.
I may talk the same
and walk the same
but thinking
is a totally different game.
I thank the Lord
for how lucky I have been
left with a weakness
in my left arm.
You see, if it had been
my right one,
it would have caused an ALARM
because I would no longer be able to write.
God has given me a gift to do his work
and share his word with others.
He patiently waits to see again.

WHAT....WHEN.....HOW?

Where am I?
How did I get here?
Why won't my brain work?
What can't I hear?
Why is it so noisy?
When did I get here?
Why is it so busy?
Why is nothing clear?

Am I in heaven?
Have I passed to the
other side?
It's busy like it is in a bloody hell.
Am I dead or alive?
Why can't I remember
how I got here?
The machines and monitors
make things clear.
The hospital bed isn't like the one
I have at home.
I'm very aware that I am not on my own
as the doctors smile.
Hey! That must be a good sign.
Why can't I remember?
I can't find my sense of humour
and is this some kind of joke?
Oh! Please God,

LOST AND FOUND ...Life After a Stroke

have I had another stroke?

Why can't I get my words out?
They are stuck in my head and in my heart.
Shouldn't they be angry
and not smiling instead?
Whenever I am here,
must I be on the mend?

Memory isn't always
ones best friend
and with my medical history,
I have become a frequent visitor.

Who cares how I got here
I am SAFE in God's hands.

WHERE???

Where are you Lord?
Please tell me.
Have I gone wrong?
You must be pretty angry
and this isn't fun.

Did I not say my prayers?
Did I do something wrong?
Did I not pray good enough?
Where Lord have you gone?

I feel like I'm being punished.
The doctors, say that I'm not.
Please Lord, I need you
but I forgot how to pray.

My faith has always been strong.
At least, it used to be
but I can't understand Lord
Why this is happening to me?

There many poorly people
here on this ward
who have also had a stroke.
I've been one of the lucky ones.
THANK YOU LORD.

I'm not sure if that
is classed as a prayer.
Lord, please Lord,
I really need to know

THAT YOU'RE THERE.

EMOTIONS

Emotionally entangled
Emotionally attached
Emotionally hungry
For any kind of feedback
Emotionally unstable
Emotionally confused
Emotionally undecided
Which path should you choose?
Emotionally under attack
Emotionally detached
Emotionally blinded
To find your way back
Emotionally empty
Emotionally never right
Emotionally drained
No fight left to fight
Emotionally speechless
Emotionally numb
Emotionally scarred
From battles not won
Emotionally …… DONE:

LET ME REST

Stop the world from turning.
Stop my brain from whirling.
Stop my stomach from churning.
Let me rest a while.

Stop my eyes from bawling.
Stop my Spirit from falling.
Stop my mouth from calling.
Let me rest a while.

Stop my body from aching.
Stop my heart from breaking.
Stop my mind from mistaking.
Let me rest a while.

Stop each thought from meaning.
Stop those words believing.
Stop my nerves from screaming.
Let me rest a while.

Stop the tears from brimming.
Stop the promises from bringing.
STOP....just....STOP everything
UNTIL
I have rested for a while.

HEY! JUST ME!!!

I have stumbled;
I have fallen;
I have picked myself up;
I have pushed people away;
I have tried being tough;
I have been no Angel.
I have been a mixture of good and bad.
I have cried when I'm happy.
I have lied when I'm sad.
I have searched to the left.
I have studied the right.
I have often made wrong choices.
When I saw no hope in sight
I have braved many mountains.
I have tackled most hills.
I have sobbed my heart out
when my feet became still.
I have witnessed the black.
I have seen the grey.
I have chased the rainbow.
Its colours showing me
another way
to find pinks, oranges and blues.
To find their destination with
my Inner Peace

through and through.
I have no doubts whatsoever
each new day I get
Jesus is with me.
MY SAFETY NET

LOST AND FOUND ... Life After a Stroke

SID

Looks like I have company
of loneliness.
I often complain since
I don't know where this one's been hiding.

I've decided Sid
will be his name.
The fact right now
I'm mega freaking out
and trying hard not to scream.

Sid is the Biggest Spider
I have ever seen.
Just strutting his stuff,
calmly walking up and down.

Nothing wrong with his self-esteem.
I have never been
a fan of creepy crawlies
and I mean ANY kind.

I reckon my kids
would be proud of me
at this moment in time.

I know God works in

mysterious ways
but answer prayers, he does.

I asked him to send me a new friend.
Looks like Sid staying is a must.
Oh heck!
Looks like Sid is off again.
I hope he doesn't come too close.
Hey, I'm really doing my best
I reckon that's better than most.Phew!!!

I need to get out more, eh!!

THE CHALLENGE

You are challenging me God
each one I accept.
My body is weary, and
my house is un kept.

You keep me going God
with your peace and overwhelming
love and trust.

It's getting harder for
my friends and family God.
They put all their faith and hopes
in Doctors, monitors and pills

They haven't found you yet God.
I pray and hope they will.
"How will they know, they ask me?"
My reply "Believe me you will."

God, you collected all
my broken pieces.
You make me complete, whole.
You never said
it would be easy
but promised I wouldn't be alone.

My greatest challenge
is to stay alive
for there is so much work
to be done.

With your Trust, Strength and Love, God
Every day Challenge No 1
Is WON.

I PRAY

I pray for the homeless
for more homes
than less.

I pray for praise to be given
for those doing their best.
I pray for the calm
before every storm.

For each life ending;
For each new born;
I pray for the blinkered as
they gain more insight.

I pray for the weak
for more strength to fight.
I pray for more employment
that they get a
fair boss.

I pray for the grieving
for each of their loss.
I pray for the poverty
everywhere along.

I pray for all ailments.

IS IT REHERSHAL OR TEST?

GOD here is another test, and
will it ever stop?
But, is this the test?
Pause a moment then,
STOP.

If, buts and maybes, the
words I often use.
With a few this and thats
which leaves me confused.

I now call them
Gods Rehearsals.
The script...Is your life
as I'm writing this
I am thinking back.
Bear with me, it may take a while.
They say God never gives you
more than you can handle,
even at your lowest ebb.
Full of pity, self-doubt, whatever, and
where had God placed you?
In my case, I was placed in a hospital bed.

Where he knew I would be rested,
Fed, medicated and restored
to cope with the next part

of my script.
Bring it on Lord.
These words, I write.
You don't have to read
It is definable not a test
but one of Gods Rehearsals.

How do I know this?
Because my writing is
at its best......the gift that God gave me.

ANOTHER

Another sleepless night;
Another early dawn;
Another painful stretch;
Another weary yawn;
Another new ache;
Another new pain;
Another 'Oh No';

Here we go again,
another hunt for the slipper.
Another shake of the head;
Another lingering look
at the uninviting bed.

Another new day;
Another new hour;
Another decision to make,
smell...or have a shower.
Another day has gone by unnoticed.
Another day passes me by.
Another mixture of emotions;
I sigh! I frown! I cry!
Another exhausting day over;
Another climb into bed;
Another, tossing and turning;
Lonely night ahead:
Another glimpse into my world.

DARKNESS V LIGHT

Where there is darkness
there is also light.
Sometimes it's dim;
Sometimes it's bright;
Sometimes it's near;
Sometimes it's far;
Maybe a candle;
Maybe a star:

The choice is ours!

Do we choose to see it?
Do we choose to stay blind?
Do we choose to follow it?
Do we choose to lag behind?
Will we get burnt if we get too near?
How else will the darkness lift
to conquer the fear?

When you see a blind person's eyes?
They are open wide.
All they see is darkness
but they don't try and hide.

They see more than we do
because deep inside,

as I always have
and God takes
care of me too.

A BIG DEAL

I got dressed today
and it's no big deal.
I have been shook up,
willing to heal.

Closing my mind and my heart
to everything.
Totally giving up Self-worth;
Self confidence; and faith.

No joke,
they use tubes to feed you.
It is no fun,
they turn you hourly
to prevent pressure sores.
They even wipe your bum.

What about the anger?
It eats me up inside.
They don't have a magic pill
So, it becomes easier to hide.

Too depressed
to get dressed.
Another day goes by
and today has been

back into my chair and
tell me it takes time.
Not hearing my pathetic excuses
you wipe those tears of mine.
So, from the bottom of my heart,
I just want to thank each of you.
A TEAM you certainly are.
You are worth your weight in gold.
I am giving you 5 Stars.
From my family and I,

We thank you so much
for all your endless support.
Letting us gain your trust
especially your Patience.
I know I'm hard work
but that bit makes you smirk.
I could go on with more and more Praise
but I have exercises to do.
Hey! why do you look
so shocked and amazed?
Did you really think
I wouldn't see them through???
At Times when I was being stubborn,
the thought must have occurred to you.
You taught me a lot
So from me to you
THANK YOU.

The following collection of poems Kari had intended to group together under the name Pathfinder. They express feelings and experiences during periods where her Christian faith was challenged and how through her writing she was able to gather spiritual strength and remain on the right path.

The Life after Stroke and Pathfinder periods of her life have a strong overlap and thus compliment each other in this one publication.

PATHFINDER

KARI THOMASON

IN BETWEEN THE LINES

DID YOU KNOW.....?

Do you know that when I write
my poetry books,
I am not depressed.

I don't have a mental Illness.
I don't pass their test
because my brain
wasn't fried by E.C.T.

I have a Voice.
It took me 40 years to find it.
With all the knowledge,
medication and stuff,
I'm leaving them way behind.

Their big long words,
intellectual stuff;
When unsure,
they throw another label at me.

Yeah right! A cure.
I write my poems
as basic as I can.
It has always been my therapy.
No bull shit.

No sugar coating.
ME just being ME.

Before you judge,
read the words.
Read between the lines,
every single word I've written.
Then, make up your mind.
I don't want praise
Or even acknowledgements.

I just want you to see.
I just want you to read
In- between the lines.
I want to be LABEL FREE.
Thank you.

YOU'RE NOT LISTENING

Here we are again.
We've been here before.
Will you save all your platitudes?

I know the score.
Because of my illness,
It is fair to say
I am up and down
like a yo yo.

It's different, day by day.
Do they think I
want to be here
taking up a bed?

When in the comfort
Of my own home
I could be instead.
A Respect DNR form
will be the last label
that I will wear.

I have been labeled all my life,
I guess one more seems fair.
I know God had his reasons
I just wish He'd make them clear.

Who can I talk too?
Questions needing answers.
Who wants to hear?
This time it's been different.

I wish I could explain.
It seems more Soul Searching.
It seems a lot more pain.
Physically...mentally...Spiritually.

I'm all at 6s and 7s.
Is it very difficult
getting a place in Heaven?
God takes me to the brim.
Then, sends me back again.

I am tired, I am weary.
No more energy left
for this game.
They are listening
but I can't utter the words.

What is the chance of me actually being heard?

They are not mind readers
and can only work with what you give.
I can't fight any more.

I <u>DO</u>N'T WANT TO LIVE

WHY?

Why don't they know
My smile is fake and not real?
Why do they try to stitch
a wound that won't heal?

Why aren't they mind readers?
Why can't they see my pain?
Why don't they have x ray vision?
Why can't they see the weight, see the strain?

Why can't they catch
each silent tear?
Why can't they shine a torch
through this tunnel of fear?

Why can't they justgo through the motions
Andpretend that they care?
I know I'm being unreasonable.
I know I'm being unfair.

How can they help me
if I won't let them in?
The bricks to my concrete wall
are now paper thin.

The one thing I had
to keep me safe.

Now I know I was foolish building it
When I thought I was being brave.

THE BOTTOM LINE LORD......?

Okay then,
I guess this is it?
Where are you now Lord?
On my bed, won't you sit?

You are most welcome.
You have free range.
My troubled thoughts
You could rearrange.

Is Heaven opened?
Is it far?
Is it hard to get into?

I have done my homework
The question is,
how will I get there?

Will I be travelling alone?
Is it everything they
have taught us?

About our New Home,
Troubled are my thoughts.
I have no Fear
because I know you are near Lord.

Could you please
send me a list?
I pray to get it right since
I'm pretty certain
I will be there tonight.

A lot of prayers
has been sent up for me.
I don't want to let people
down.
I'm not asking for a miracle
Just a break....
Lord, Please come for me
and take me......HOME.

I'm so tired Lord and
I can't do this anymore.
Abba, come get your little girl.
She just can't fight any more.

SO SO TIRED

BORROWED TIME

This is the 7th poem,
I have started to write.
I can't seem to reach the end.
Each one very different
from the last.

Is this the end?
I make people smile;
I cheer them up;
It's what I love to do.

Why should anyone
have to go it alone?
Why go through the darkness alone?

The people never see
the pain that I am in
Or the fear, I constantly hide.
I always say "See you soon...."
Never parting with a goodbye,

I always tell them.
"Dry your tears and move on..."
Where they will go, I wonder
When I am gone?

At last, my poem is nearly at the end.

Self pity, it is not.
I just wanted a hug and
a few kind words.
Why am I thinking of the flower?

For-Get-Me-Not.

CHASING A RAINBOW

I am chasing a rainbow
Does it mean a total impossible
farfetched dream?

I am chasing a rainbow, of
colours that make my heart melt
like a snowflake on the tongue.

Oh! It's so heartfelt.
I am chasing a rainbow.
I am in no rush.
Why wait for a downpour?

The wind can give it a gentle nudge.
I am chasing a rainbow.
I have no fear.
Its beauty lets me know
that God is near.

I am chasing a rainbow.
Only a few know where
I am coming from.
Listen to the words
of my favourite song

Somewhere Over the Rainbow.

CHANGE

I feel I am at a crossroads,
and a change is taking place.
I hope that it's a positive one
and I don't fall flat on my face.

If I fall on my face,
I will do what I normally do.
I will pick myself up, dust myself off,
and then hide in the loo.

I am not feeling too apprehensive;
If anything, a little confused.
Will the change be physical or emotional?
Will I even get to choose?

I hope it includes lots of laughter
Belly wobbles aches and giggles.
You know the one where
even if you cross your legs
You still manage to piddle.

I wish that I could still party,
let my hair down, have a blast.
I not sure my back would hold up to it
Or my nebulizers would last.

Yes, here I am at a crossroads

with not even a map insight.
I probably couldn't read it anyway.
Can you now see my plight?

ERM...this poem was meant to be serious
Deep....meaningful, all of that stuff.
Hey! Maybe that's the change taking place.
I'm not light hearted enough.

You could always call my bluff.

BUTTONS

I use to have a reject button.
Trust me, shiny and new
is every problem in my life.
My button got well used.

A lot like a comforter
or a dummy, as parents call them today.
No one could wean me of it
because it was secretly
hidden away.

I'm not even sure
how I got it.
Was I small or fully grown?
Was it passed onto me?
Was it handmade?
Its history was unknown.

It came in handy
when I had no voice.
It gave me control.
It gave me the choice.

Sadly, yes, I also chose its name.
Reject Button
until my eyes were opened,
I asked if God

had a reject button?
These words were spoken.

No Kari, he doesn't
just open up your heart.
He has been patiently waiting for you,
his creation, from the start.
He won't take your button from you
but will be there.

To let you know you're safe,
He will never ever reject you.
He rolls out the safety net in its place as
I brought my button out of hiding.
To say I wasn't nervous
would be a lie.

With the honesty and love,
They had spoken and
all I could do was cry.

I walked out of church lighter
but my button
had been a big part of my life.
It's now replaced with another button
This one, I named PAUSE.

Not hidden, but used often
mainly when I need

time Out with God.
When I am lost and weary
and not sure what to do.
I just press my Pause Button
and hear him say
"Child.....I have got you".

TIME OUT

I'm giving God a break
a well-earned rest.
Although my thoughts are negative,
I am doing my best.

When I prayed for his ears
to get better
I forgot to add a P S.
If I was out of the equation,
Perhaps, the word wouldn't be
in such an awful mess.

I know these words
will anger a lot
but they come from the heart.
This is between me and God.
I know a negative start.

Hey, don't think I no longer love him,
or that my Faith has ceased.
My motto 'Carers need Care too.
That includes God, I believe.

The Greatest Carer of all,
the Main Man who is always there
to catch me when I stumble and fall.
But I feel I am being unfair.

He has the whole world
to take Care off.
Yeo! Then there's me
demanding instead of listening.
Just so full of negativity.

So I'm him giving a break
A well-earned rest
P.S God. I'm doing my best.

DIFFERENCES

Look at me,
what do you see?
Is it black or is it white?
Is it a bit of both?

Let's start with my hair.
It is purple
The colour is loud
and bold.

IT IS THE COLOUR

Many thoughts unfold.
White hair speaks Wisdom.
Grey speaks old.
A perm gone wrong
shouts afro, I'm told.

Just a word.
describes a style,
unlocking loads of emotions
that will travel miles.
Before we know it,
It brings us back to race.

Now, let's move away from hair and
concentrate on the face.

Mine is full of freckles.
Did I have a choice?
In the height of summer,
They determined my voice.
They literally cover my face and made
it hard to tell.

What was my race?
I got bullied
And beyond doubt
I wanted to learn more.
What is all the hate was about?

I approached my old school books for
answers I hoped they'd give.
I did old fashion research in libraries.
I went way back and researched
how generations lived.

No simple answers
Or solutions, it seems.
It was patently obvious
that any colour
would determine their dreams.

Labels had been attached.
It seems from the beginning of time,

the world didn't stand a chance.
Take for example,
our reading habits today.
Loneliness versus Romance;
What are we teaching our young ones?
We're not 'Google' takes care of that
as a Human Race.
It is not about the devices
Xbox, Tablet or Mobile Phone.
Not all parents can afford that.

HUMAN being is the keyword.
Love is the keyword.
The power of speech
and the freedom enlivens us

Today, no one gets heard;
WHY?
Because everyone is pigeon holed.
Each word is picked at
and pulled apart
whether it comes from within.
Regardless of the colour of your skin
It should come from the heart.
We were all created
by the same man.
He forgave each of our sins

and nowhere in my research did it show
He was COULORBLIND.
He lets everyone in.

I wonder again
where all this HATE came from?
I know this poem
will anger a lot
but he gave me the gift to write.

WE are all Brothers and Sisters.
TOGETHER WE MUST FIGHT
RACISM.

THE STOPWATCH

Smiling,
I am thinking
of my sports teacher
and the stopwatch in her hand.

I hardly ever saw her use it
and I couldn't understand.
She carried it with her everywhere.
It seemed a big part of her life
because I seldom saw her use it.

I just had to ask her why.
It's an inquisitive question
from an inquisitive mind.

I think I was about six
I asked if it was broken
and needed to be fixed?
Then, she began to tell me
about its history.
Her story began to unfold.
Everyone who carried
the Stopwatch had once
been a troubled Soul.

When she received hers
She had thrown all caution

to the wind.
She knew the Maker
was very important
but she didn't BELIVE in him.

She didn't want to be responsible
taking care of something
so precious and rare.
Her heart was too heavy.
Her world was too dark.
She'd learnt early

to no longer care.
What use to her
would a stopwatch be?

At the age of nine,
placed in her hand was stories she told.
It would be repeated throughout time.
Whenever you burden through life, and
the pain you can no longer bare,
press the button on The Stopwatch.
Call my name and I will be there.

The story of the Stopwatch,
each time, must be told.
Use it also as a compass
to rescue more troubled Souls
from childhood.

Through to old age
Each prayer will be heard.
Gods Timing is Perfect
and his WORD
as I turn my Stopwatch
in my hand.

Once again, I smile.
I know a lot of troubled Souls.
The Stopwatch story
they need to hear.
It is worth all its weight in Gold.
It will travel the miles.

MY AWESOME GOD

I know my God is Awesome.
He is also a busy man but
He never, ever turns a deaf ear.

He has a sense of humour
as well as his serious side.
He keeps us all in place and
never leaves our side.

Sadly, it is us that leave him.
Yet, patiently he waits.
He helps us to find our way back.

When we dump on him
all our anger, shame and hate
he never forsake us.

I was the biggest Runner
every chance I could take
until it became obvious
that It was my biggest mistake.

Pause for just a moment.
Whatever you are doing now, STOP.
Just 5 minutes out of your day
Surely, God deserves that.

I use to be so quick with excuses.
Oh! Plenty I could find.
I would challenge him
but not wait for an answer.

Just moved on to my next demand
Yet, God never did a Runner.
When they got out of hand,
Somehow, he'd let me know
He had heard me.
He would always be there.

We didn't always come
to the same conclusion
after each off my prayers.
HE WAS ALWAYS FAIR
Yes! My God is Awesome.
Yes! Now I understand.
My Yesterday's, Today's and Tomorrow's;
He holds safely in his hands.

MY COMMITMENT

"On a hill far away
stood an Old Rugged Cross...."
It is one of my favourite Hymns.

Searching my heart,
Mind and Soul
making me accountable for all of my sins.

This Selfless man,
who shed his blood;
A sacrifice he did make.

With no hesitation,
only unconditional Love
So a place at his side I could take.

The Baptism Water
will deeply cleanse me.
My old ill-fitting clothes
I will shed.

I rise whole with my new clothes.
It Will be a perfect fit.
From that day on,
I will walk the walk.

My head I will hold high
and I will, forever
praise his name
Until the day I die.

THE COMPASS

Every picture tells a story.
If I could paint,
I would tell you this.

Don't underestimate the compass.
IT is accurate,
no hit and miss.

Now, I have no sense of direction
within the compass.
I was an expert at getting lost.
It causes great amusement
for all the world to see.

It would be a mistake
to ask me for directions.
I would say
follow that bus or car.
Oh! You would get there eventually.
You will make a full round trip
that wasn't that far.

If you followed my eyes
instead of my hands,
the only way is UP
where God waits patiently
for you to declare your love.

If you do need a compass,
He will guide you
should you get lost.

Without rules or regulations,
It is clear God is the boss.

No parking tickets
Or speed limits
Just a special journey,
"You and Him".

Don't be afraid.
Just open wide your heart
and let your journey begin.

THE ONLY WAY IS UP.

THE KEYRING

I hear the jingle
of my keys.
It makes me smile.

Attached to my keyring
It proves that Hope
travel miles.

When I received my keyring
I was down and out.
Being Homeless was nothing to shout about/

I was handed a warm blanket
for the winter
to help me cope.

In the blanket, was my keyring of hope.
Attached to it was a note.
Was it meant to be there?

Suddenly, I felt lighter.
Somebody did care.

I read out aloud the verse
that had been
written in faded ink.

LOST AND FOUND ...Life After a Stroke

I am no longer worried
about what the others think.
Most of them were not here
by their own choice
But I knew that I was.

I ignored the voice.
All the bad stuff that had happened,
there was only one man to blame.
In my ignorance, I couldn't

Say aloud his name.
I knew then the words written
was not a verse, but a prayer.
I repeated over and over again.
Praying...
"Please God, please be there.

When I awoke four days later
on a hospital bed
They had been warned
that I probably wouldn't make it but
I proved them wrong, instead.

I asked for my keyring
and heard the jangle of keys

"Thank You God," I whispered
They had found a new home for me.

WONDERING

Nana, is Grand Dad
really in heaven with God?
Are they taking good care
of Patch my dog?

Do you think Jesus
hears my prayers?
I can't see him
anywhere.

Some grown ups
tells us stories
that don't always make sense.
I try really hard to listen
like when I'm climbing a big fence.

Some grown-ups cry
When they hear Gods name.
Some sing and dance
like on one of my computer games.

Like they teach us,
I still say my prayers.
Ending with a P.S.

Jesus, are you there......?

BLIND SPOT

Is it possible in your Faith?
You can have a stubborn streak?
Doubting, giving up
when prayers and answers don't meet.

Lets pause for a moment,
think about this.
I know I'm certainly guilty
of this one.

There are times when I should be
turning to God
sometimes the opposite
direction, I run.

In my heart I feel
I am totally committed.
The crisis comes my way and
I am very quick
to ask for Gods help
and guidance on that day
when the answer is not
the solution I hoped for.

How quick I am to question why?
Lack of patience, lack of trust.
Each emotion, I cannot deny.

I call this my Blind spot.
I must erase it, and
pray for more patience.

I must trust and stay faithful
believing only in the
Man who knows.

GOD

A PEP TALK

Dear Lord, can we have
one of our chats.
It's nothing too serious.
It is me seeking some quiet
alone with you.

You have always been
a great comfort to me.
I am a little concerned
I'm not praying hard enough.

Please don't mistake this
as doubting your Eternal Love,
Do I make too many demands or
requests that dashes my...hopes?

This thought makes it sometimes difficult
for me to cope.
Maybe, I don't thank you enough
for each answered prayer.
I know I am guilty of that one
much too much to my despair.

I know I get negative
And I work myself up
trying not to undo
everything you have done.

Well Lord, thanks for the chat
I guess I'll get going.
Never doubting, always knowing
I am your CHILD.
Thank you for loving me.

HE'S ALWAYS WITH ME

I use my writing
as my therapy.
I'm known to tell it how it is.
Not to win popularity contests
trust me it's far from this.

It's better than any medication.
The results are safe and calm
even with electric shock treatment
which causes less good- more harm.

They say it causes short term memory loss
as well as my name.
I forgot I could write
Alcohol and self-harming took over
each scar out of sight and
each one story.

Then, I discovered country 'n' western music.
In most songs someone died
despair, heartache, well it didn't matter.
Once again, I learnt how to cry.

I knew I had to channel my pain
and somehow learn again, to fight,

to find my voice.
Yes I had a choice.

So, I began again to write.

I was introduced to God at an early age
about God and how did I feel?
Well I never saw his face
If he didn't show up He couldn't be real.

They told us he was everywhere.
Then, magic he must be.
The above was my thoughts at the age of six
when locked in the chapel

To say sorry to him
for something bad
that I didn't do.
But hey, that didn't seem to matter
each time this happened.
I truly knew
my image of God was indeed shattered.

Oh, I gave God the benefit of the doubt.
I had convinced myself he was deaf
He seemed to listen
to my Jailors.

The priests and the nuns were
locked in the chapel.

I was left
growing up and sure I had doubts.

Brainwashed I think it's called now.
I was definitely confused
but very aware.
I wasn't alone, somehow.

I still said my prayers
as we were taught.
To a man I still could not see.
I prayed for his ears
to get better.
Then, waited to see if he heard me.

I can honestly say
that he did.
Still an appearance he didn't make
but I'm older now.
Taught differently somehow
learning from my mistakes.

He may not have made an appearance
but he had definitely taken control.

In every aspect of my life
even when I was not as good as gold.

I was good enough for him
not to abandon me
but to give me the gift to write.

I know I tell it how it is
and don't always get it right.

Words can be so powerful
but please make no mistake.
I'm not a teacher or a preacher.
I pray I never dictate.

Thank you for reading.
This to the end.
Not all the words come from me.
Work that one out
then without a doubt.

God is everyone's friend
not just me
and the best kind of Therapy.

NEVER

Never underestimate
the power of prayer.
I do it often
much to my despair.

When you think God isn't listening
Negative thoughts take over your mind.
This happens all too often.
Is my Faith blind?

The way they say Love can be
I often get confused.
I wonder if he gets mad with me.
At the worst, amused,

I often start my prayers
in a negative way.
Like "Ok Lord,
What's the score?
Are you even hearing me?
How can I be sure?"

Then, out of the blue
when I think I'm alone
He lets me know
that he's always been there
and will be until I'm called home.

OPEN

Open your arms
and let him in.
He gives the best cuddles.
Win   Win Win

Open your soul,
He is always near
with Pure Unconditional Love
catching every tear.

Open your mind,
He is never far away.
He always listens.
He hears every prayer.

Open your heart
even when you go astray.
He waits patiently.
HE NEVER RUNS AWAY.

Open your mouth
and say
THANK YOU JESUS
For another new day.

I AM TRYING

Jesus, I know you're here with me
but I feel I'm letting you down.
My mood is low and
my stress levels high.

I'm trying hard
to turn things around.
I really do love you
with all my heart
and soul.

I truly do believe.
Please tell me,
What is wrong with me?
Why haven't you
given up on me?

Each night in prayer
I make a promise to you.
I will try harder
to do better in serving you.
Why can't I get it right?
I AM TRYING.

TO ANYONE WHO'S LISTENING?

Ahhh! My body is so weary.
Just put me out too rest in
a Nursing Home
or knackers Yard.

Whichever you thing best,
I didn't make it
to Church today;
To Worship, and shout
a heartfelt Amen.

To be honest Am
struggling to hold this pen,
Ahhh! My body is weary.
It comes to us all in time.

For those of you,
Who think I sound about 90,
I will be 60 in 2 years time.

You're only a young UN
I hear you all say
Then, please send
some of your energy my way.

Remove all my aches.

Make the pain go.
Wind me up like a robot.
Make me go faster, not slow.

Please re programme my brain
for pain free thoughts.
My sense of humour at
A charity shop, could be bought.

I'm deciding now.
Should I post this poem?

It could turn out to be a curse.
I could get carrots sent
or even batteries sent.
Just don't send a Bloody Hearst.

Thanks for listening

VOTE OF THANKS

Thanks everyone for your endless love through the times of trouble.
I am even stronger because I am a part of an important family.
With the greatest love and kindness you have inspired me. A thousand thanks.

Best regards.

Kari Thomason

ABOUT THE AUTHOR

Kari Thomason has been writing poetry for over 50 years, and has often been heard referring it to be her therapy. In sharing her work, all she hopes to achieve is to reach others.

After her last book was published Kari announced, due to ill health, that she wouldn't be doing any more books, it seems that God has a different idea.

Thus - Lost and Found (Life after a stroke) is her new book.

Kari had a stroke 3 years ago, and is speaking from personal experience.

She lost her dignity, confidence and yes, at a very low point. She lost her FAITH too.

Eventually, all of those things she found again, hence the title off her book! It was a long, slow hard journey, but it is DO ABLE.

YOU ARE NOT ON YOUR OWN

Printed in Great Britain
by Amazon